My Healthy Life

Eating Well

Ryan Wheatcroft   Katie Woolley

PowerKiDS press

Published in 2024 by The Rosen Publishing Group, Inc.
2544 Clinton Street, Buffalo, NY 14224

Editor: Victoria Brooker
Designer: Anthony Hannant, Little Red Ant

Cataloging-in-Publication Data

Names: Woolley, Katie, author. | Wheatcroft, Ryan, illustrator.
Title: Eating well / by Katie Woolley, illustrated by Ryan Wheatcroft.
Description: New York : Powerkids Press, 2024. | Series: My healthy life |
Includes glossary and index.
Identifiers: ISBN 9781642827439 (pbk.) | ISBN 9781642827446 (library bound) |
ISBN 9781642827453 (ebook)
Subjects: LCSH: Food habits--Juvenile literature. | Nutrition--Juvenile literature.
Classification: LCC RA784.W665 2024 | DDC 613.2--dc23

Manufactured in the United States of America

CPSIA Compliance Information: Batch #CSPK24. For further information contact Rosen Publishing at 1-800-237-9932.

Contents

You Are What You Eat!

Eating is something we do every day. The food you eat and the water you drink keeps you alive. Food and water help your body to think, grow, move, and breathe.

Everyone needs to eat a balanced diet every day. This gives your body the nutrients it needs to stay healthy. Food can be put into food groups. You need to eat a little bit from each group to have a balanced diet.

Where Does Your Food Go?

As soon as you put food into your mouth it begins to be digested as you chew it. Digestion is the breaking down of food. Once your food enters your stomach, it mixes with acids that turn it into a thick liquid.

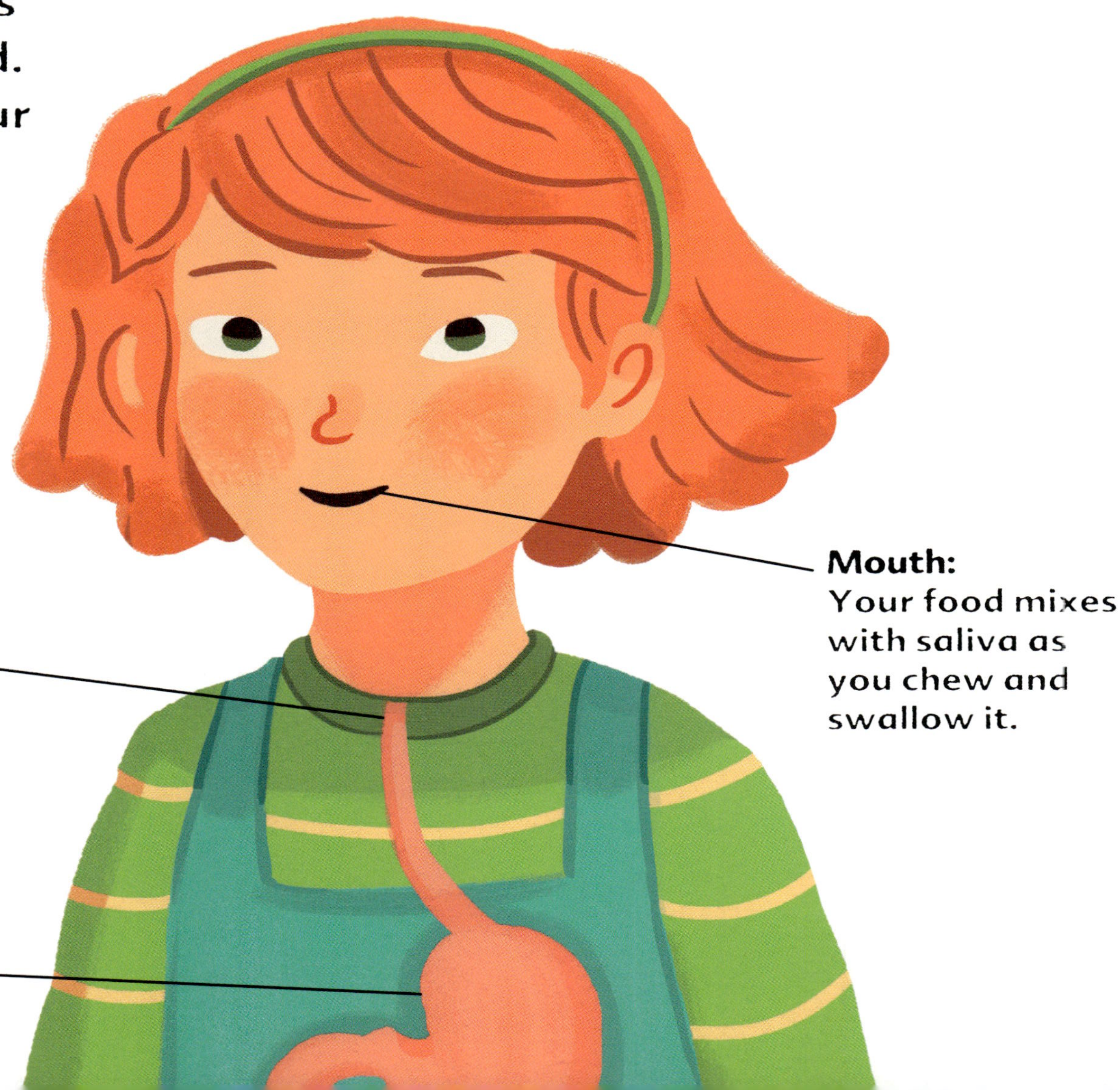

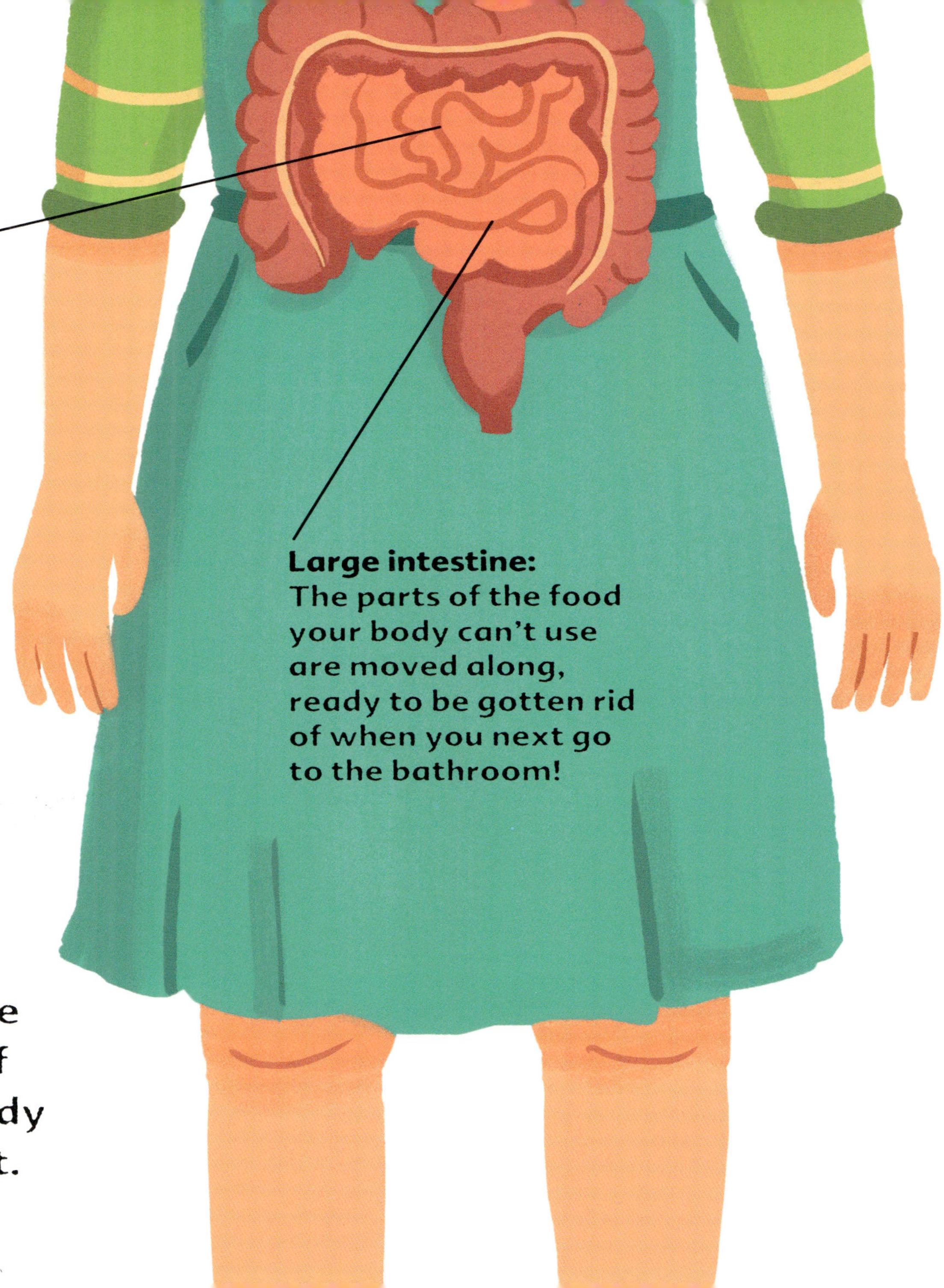

This liquid in your stomach moves into your intestines. Your small intestine absorbs the nutrients from the food. Your large intestine leads the unused parts of your food out of your body when you go to the toilet.

What Are Vitamins and Minerals?

Vitamins and minerals are substances found in food. Your body needs vitamins to work properly and to help you grow. Each vitamin does an important job. For example, vitamin C, found in fruit and vegetables, helps your skin to heal if you get a cut.

Your body uses minerals to perform different jobs, too. Calcium is a mineral that helps to build strong bones. The mineral iron, found in red meat and green vegetables, helps take oxygen from your lungs to the rest of your body.

Carbohydrates

Carbohydrates can be found in starchy foods such as bread, potatoes, cereals, and pasta. Carbohydrates give your body most of its energy needs. This energy is slowly released to keep you fuller for longer.

Protein

Your body needs protein to grow, build, and repair itself. It helps makes your bones strong and healthy. You get protein from foods such as meat, fish, nuts, beans, seeds, eggs, and cheese.

Milk and Dairy

Milk and dairy contain calcium, which helps to keep your bones and teeth healthy. Foods such as cheese and yogurt are all made from milk and dairy. Your body needs about three portions of milk and dairy every day.

Fruit and Vegetables

Your body needs at least five portions of fruit and vegetables every day. A portion of fruit or vegetables is about the same size as the palm of your hand. Each portion contains lots of vitamins and minerals to keep your body healthy.

Fats

Your body needs essential fats to grow, but not too much! Fatty foods give you energy, help your body absorb some vitamins, and protect your nervous system.

Unsaturated fats can be good for your heart. They can be found in nuts, seeds, avocados, and oily fish.

Saturated fats, found in meat, butter, and cream, give us energy but not many nutrients. Your body needs less of this type of fat.

Sugar

The sugar you eat is a kind of carbohydrate. Eating sugary foods can make you feel full for a while, but you're missing out on important nutrients that are in healthier foods. Too much sugar is also bad for your teeth. Having sugary foods as a treat is okay as part of a balanced diet.

Water

Water helps your brain and body to function. The healthiest drinks are water and milk, as these don't contain extra sugar that can damage your teeth.

The amount of water you need depends on your age, the weather, and how much exercise you do. Try to drink between six and eight glasses a day.

Ready, Set, Breakfast!

Eating breakfast gives your body the energy it needs to begin the day. You'll be less tired and grumpy and be able to concentrate more when you've had something to eat.

What you eat in the morning is important. Eating foods that contain whole grain, fiber, and protein such as cereals, oatmeal, and eggs are all good for you. What is your favorite breakfast food?

Lunchtime Pit Stop

When your stomach starts to rumble during the day, your body is telling you that it's time to eat. A busy morning of exercise, learning, and playing will have used up the energy you got from your breakfast. It's time to refuel and stop for lunch!

A healthy lunch doesn't need to be boring! Choosing some colorful fruit and vegetables, your favorite sandwich filling on whole-grain bread, and a glass of milk are all delicious ways to enjoy a healthy lunch.

Dinner Is Served!

Dinner is just as important a meal for your body as breakfast and lunch, as it's the last meal you will eat before bed. A dinner packed with healthy carbohydrates and proteins will fill you up and help you get a good night's sleep.

You can cook together in the kitchen and share stories about your day.

Sitting down for a meal at the end of the day is also a chance to catch up with your family.

Snack Attack!

Your body needs refueling in between breakfast, lunch, and dinner—especially if you have been really active. Feeling hungry in between meals can make you feel tired and grumpy, so it is a good idea to eat a healthy snack.

A piece of fruit will give you energy. You could have some raw vegetables, such as carrots and cucumber, with hummus or soft cheese. You could even make a smoothie with berries, yogurt, and a banana.

Ditch the Junk!

Some foods that are high in fat, sugar, and salt but low in nutrients and vitamins are often called junk foods. Chips, fries, cookies, and soda are all junk foods. They might taste nice but it's best to have them as a treat every once in a while.

These kinds of foods give you a quick energy boost but that energy is soon used up and you'll feel tired and hungry again. If you choose something healthy instead, you'll have more energy and feel happier.

Top Tips!

Mix it up! Don't get bored from eating the same thing every day. Eating lots of different kinds of foods gives your body a variety of nutrients.

Try to eat two or three portions of food packed with protein every day. For example, you could have a tuna sandwich or scrambled eggs.

Avoid fatty foods, especially at night. They are harder to digest and can keep you from getting a good night's sleep.

It's important to stay hydrated. Have a bottle of water or glass of milk when you start to feel thirsty.

It's great fun cooking your own food, too. Ask a grown-up if you can help make a meal.

Parents' and Teachers' Notes

This book is designed for young readers to begin to learn about the importance of being healthy, and the ways in which we can look after our bodies by eating well. Read the book with children either individually or in groups. Don't forget to talk about the pictures as you go.

Eating well and having a balanced diet doesn't mean eating boring food. There are lots of different kinds of foods to try. Learning to eat well is very important, as a healthy diet will help children grow, play, and learn. Here are some discussion topics to encourage further thinking about eating well:

- Can you think of three reasons why it's important to eat well?
- Talk about the word "healthy." What do you think it means to be healthy?
- Different nutrients help keep different parts of your body healthy. What does calcium do? What does protein do?

- Why are foods with lots of fat and sugar bad for you?
- Talk about your favorite foods. Are they healthy or should they just be a treat?

Activities you can do:

- Use empty food packaging to complete your own food plate collage.
- Try making your own fruit smoothie as a healthy snack.

Further reading

Can I Have a Snack? by Helena Markham (Rosen, 2019)
Eating Healthy Foods by R. J. MacReady (Cavendish Square, 2022)
Powerful Protein by John Wood (Enslow, 2021)

Glossary

bloodstream the blood circulating through the body of a person or animal

fiber a material in food that helps move food through the body during the digestion process

minerals substances that help the body to grow and be healthy

nervous system a system of nerves and cells in the body that carries messages from the brain to various parts of the body

nutrients substances that help the body to grow and be healthy

portion an amount of food that is needed for one person

starchy foods foods that are high in starch and are a good source of energy. Starch is a substance found in some food we eat, such as cereal, bread, and potatoes.

whole grain made with, or containing, the whole, unprocessed grains of something

Index